TALES
FROM
Missouri

VOL. 2

VOL. 2

STANLEY TOWNSEND

CITIOFBOOKS, INC.
3736 Eubank NE Suite A1
Albuquerque, NM 87111-3579
www.citiofbooks.com
Hotline: 1 (877) 389-2759
Fax: 1 (505) 930-7244

Ordering Information:
Quantity sales. Special discounts are available on quantity purchases by corporations, associations, and others. For details, contact the publisher at the address above.

Printed in the United States of America.

ISBN-13:   Softcover   979-8-90124-235-3
                eBook   979-8-90124-236-0

Library of Congress Control Number:

TABLE OF CONTENTS

Introduction

i

These are new set of stories that make for each chapter . In my past I have written eight manuscripts and then lost them in a bad fire on Friday April 5,2025. That was caused by a wicked lighting bolt that destroyed my home. But never my dreams in writing and faith. Which became much stronger because of it.

CHAPTER ONE

Dedicated to my friend "Artie"

US MARSHAL ARTIE " MEANEST BEAR "

In the history of US Marshall's there was one man who was a legend and never to be forgotten. For this man all alone cleaned up a town and village in the territory of Oklahoma. Then without warning vanished into the Ozark Mountains and was never seen. Now a mystery begins when there was a very large amount of money that was overdue back pay long overdue for this one man.

That got the legendary Bass Reeves himself to find out more about this great man. Who alone worked for Free for thirty years without cashing a month's pay. Now a mystery begins when Mr. Reeves started reading the written records of this one man, was a full blood Cherokee and had a really mean streak in him. That is why he had the native name " Meanest Bear ".

In the year 1875, I became a Marshall and I was assigned to the territory of Oklahoma. I had to write down everything so I could be paid. The pay was great to me, over 200 dollars a month in gold. That is the money I earned, Well I kept and only used it in a have to basis.

Then I noticed that my pay was going to be wired to a bank and this really made me so very MAD at the world.

Out of my own bitter rage and having to deal with a bank. I begin to work off the side cleaning' up the very worst of towns for a small price in a way. That a new sheriff can come in and keep the peace. This never interfered with my Marshall job and that came up always first.

Then one day I got a telegraph from the Main headquarters that I was needed in the village of Kirby that was on the border of a native reservation. There was a whole lot of trouble when I came in. For my very sharp eyes seen a man getting ready to shoot me down without warning. So, I got my 45/70 Sharps rifle and nailed him dead. While in the small town there were people that became scared to come out in the open. The preacher was talking about a man with a white horse. How did he know that my horse was white.

There was mob presence in the village, and the native people were treated very badly. This really got my mean streak going and doing what is right. It was the outlaw gang that was trying so hard to get to two native women. Their purpose was very evil to them and " I was so very mad and took them on and dropped all of, right dead in their tracks.

This made the village very mad at me, and they all wanted me out of town very fast. So, I got a whiskey bottle and tried to drink away my sorrows. That is when the two native women came to me. One said "Marshall

Artie, Thank You for saving our lives and then there was a second one who really wanted me in the romantic stuff. That is when I realized that the native women were TWINS.

This was very rare thing happening to me for they alone were very beautiful, and I dropped my whiskey bottle and said to myself. "NO MORE WHISKEY"

Both native women took me around the corner and 15 minutes later, I was no longer called "Meanest Bear". I became very happy and wanted so much to be with them. Their father was the Chief and he also wanted me to be the son-in-law just right for his twin daughters. I had to take both and there will be a native marriage. Both maidens took very good care of me, and I went into the mountains just to be with them. That is when I stopped taking the 200 dollars a month and just let it sit in the bank.

That is why I never took any more money for my time being a marshal. I kept my family safe and thought of them so much. My own love for my children was always first before me. The maidens blessed me well in giving me 12 children and it was six sons and six daughters. One of my sons I named him " Great Chief " for he wanted to record and keep all records of the old ways. At first, I didn't want no part of it, but when I faced a threat to have my own kids taken away from me. Right then I gave up being a US Marshall, to me "Family comes first!"

Mr. Bass Reeves read this incredible story and was moved by the devotion of one man. Then he found a young man named "GREAT CHIEF" and presented the maidens with a check for $ 35,000.00 that was in the bank at Mosby and there will be no hate toward them.

Both maidens had the money moved to begin the first native own bank. That still stands to this day and one man who was named " GREAT CHIEF "had a son who loved flying like an eagle. He to also been blessed in having the same name. Later this man will become a hero for all time.

THE END

CHAPTER TWO

A GUNSLINGER NAMED " DARREN "

There was a book that was handwritten by the wife of a gunslinger. Telling all about her very famous man in her own life who alone took a stand for what was right. At a time of wildness and when there was no justice what's so ever. For anyone who was innocent and young at that time and now, she begins to write about the one man who was to be her only true love.

In the year 1866 right after that very terrible war was over. I was on a wagon train heading west along with a group of my lady friends. All of us ladies sold out of our land for a guide and a gunslinger to follow us. Then about a quarter way there they left all of us alone. To fend for ourselves and that became a fight for our own survival. Then winter was coming and that made our lives even worse to be. They left us in an old home and there was a running stream of water close by. That was to be the only light of hope in this very wicked time. All of us ladies pulled together and began to make this homework for us. Then the signs of fall were coming and there was no sight of a man anywhere.

On a very cold fall day a man finally showed up upon our door. He was weakened by the loss of the main things food and water and was so very tired. Then he went out and all of us ladies carried him to the only bed in this home. Then we took turns to help him recover. Then May, the oldest lady who was in charge, found his ID and name. Then she started talking all about him, Darren Holiday I am an ex-soldier of the confederacy now a man searching for peace. So, I did write this handwritten note, and it will say this to remind me.

I am so tired of war and always fighting and now just looking for peace in my final days here. I need it so much to put my own terrible past behind me.

May was touch by this southern gentleman note, but it was me that was taken by this great man. But it was a dreaded gunfight with a group of outlaws. They were trying to get the upper hand. May held the high ground and now the worst outlaw of them all.

"Ben The Kid" who alone was the very worst of them. He got his Asian hands-on Bridget the youngest lady in our group. That brought out the Darren Holiday to fight the whole outlaw gang it looked like all by himself. But May got his back and now the stage was set for a showdown.

SHOWDOWN

Ben the Kid was not in a great mood and wanted so much to have his way. To the young lady "Bridget" that wasn't right and then. Darren just shot him right between the eyes and the kid was no more. For he dropped dead and fear spread among the outlaws. That this one man was so freaky fast with a pistol then May traded him pistol for a golden boy Henry that was loaded and ready. Jerry the funny man of the outlaw group stopped laughing for this time it was very serious. Then Darren said this to all "All women shall be respected and given honor that was so very lost, Because of the unforgiven war of the past`. Then all the outlaws left in a hurry and never wanted to mess with or have any dealings with "Darren Holiday", then Lili Lee writes down the ending of this tale.

Darren got all of us ladies to come with him into the next town and we all settled into a boarding house. To begin a new life in the west, there was two horses that looked alike and was tied to the hitching post. Darren got on to his horse and went on his way, but that one man took my dang gum horse.

"Grouchy Ass" this one horse was trained to throw other people off, if they got on her back. She was so used to me riding her and know of this signal. Later this trick will come in to be for me, When I was trying to catch up to this man of mystery. Then I remembered my trick and called out loud. "Grouch Ass I am not on you"

Suddenly the horse threw Darren off into a deep cold creek and this time. He was so MAD at the world, just when he got out of the water. Darren wanted so much to shoot my only horse and that is when I got into action and just flashed him my heavenly body. Then he said to me, "Darling this is the only gunfight I am going to lose and pay for it dearly. I see my own horse and, I sure do need to apologize for my act of dishonor."

" Can we make an agreement to talk this matter out of a warm fire "

Lili ---------------------- I agree to his only request and from that one bad time in that cold creek. Well in a year of proper dating, I married that gunslinger and we now are living quite well. Darren Holiday and I are in love to this day. This man has seen how beautiful I am and for the horses there was three, because my horse Grouch Ass and Darren Horse had another colt and we both named him. "Silver"

CHAPTER THREE

The Adventures of Nathan Barron

Here is a story about a man who just got caught by a beautiful woman. For his love of pro football got him to walk down the aisle of marriage. He never regrets the choice made at this time. Nathan Barron was working with his best friend named Wendell and they both owned a sports shop that was all things sports.

Wendell was in charge of the books and he kept them right. Until one great day a beautiful lady came in the store looking for Nathan Barron, she had two football tickets in her hands. She was determined to give those tickets to him.

That caused Wendell to say "He is not here Miss "! Can you leave them here and I will put them in the safe right now. The beautiful lady said "Yes you may place them in your safe, because these tickets are rare and very special indeed. So, she left the sports store and Wendell winds up saying "WOW" that lucky guy and my best friend to be blessed with this stroke of good luck. That lady whom came in was so " Hot " and all I can do here is wish only the very best for her. Well it's because I am still married to my wife and while my best friend Nathan is single.

Nathan Barron came into the sports shop and was always in a hurry. Then Wendell tried to talking to him. All he ever got was ignored until it came clear for action. There was a swimming pool running and Nathan was walking by it. Then Wendell got the idea of throwing Nathan in the very cold pool just to get his attention.

It happened Nathan Barron went into the pool headfirst and came out so very mad. Already in a foul mood because his smart phone got ruined. Then a very beautiful lady came to Nathan's side with a towel to help him dry off. Her name was Maryse Delia and she was sole the owner of the football tickets. She really wanted so much to go out with this man on a date. Wendell was so surprised by the beautiful lady wanting to go on a date with Nathan, Then he looked at her and starting to stutter and went right back into the cold pool for a reality check. Now he is out of the cold pool and went toward the back room.

No beautiful woman wanted to go out on a date with me. Nathan quoted to himself just to get a grip won why his own love life just turned around. He got a bad idea about his friends playing a very mean joke on him. But it was Maryse Delia won this man over, When she and Nathan was alone in the back room of the store. Nathan Barron was drying himself off with a towel. Maryse closed the door and surprised this man by raising her own top just to get his whole attention and it worked.

Nathan and Maryse are dating now and the past adventures of the cold pool. Became history that was not forgotten. This one man alone thanked GOD for the greatest treasure he has ever received the love of his life Maryse Delia.

CHAPTER FOUR

Legacy

This story is about life and one-man personal choice to leave something behind. It happened to a very famous writer of great books. When he was approached by his children they both this, "DAD what is the meaning of Legacy "! We both have to book a report on this and present it in front of the classroom.

Well, this writer made time out of his busy schedule to help his kids. So, he called their schools for a future speaking date. Both schools were very happy to hear this one man talk even for a hour. It was a free deal, and they had nothing to lose. On the day of meeting both kids had to get their book report ready to read out loud and they didn't get it done. Their teacher was so mad at them until he showed up at class, and he talked to all at hand.

He said "Teacher here is the book report you asked for, I 've just forgotten to place it in their back packs. "! I am sorry for my own mistake here.

Teacher ---------- "It's" ok and I need to apologize to you sir for my own mistake on my end here. Now please tell us all about Destiny and what it means.

So, the very famous writer begins to speak about something very important to all of us.

DESTINY

All of us do leave something behind and that is when our own history comes alive. The paths we do lead to greatness will define us as one, to have taken in this way to be. For people who do look at our own deeds will always say. "His own destiny was to write great stories and poems"

Then the teacher said to the class. "For his own work made this world a much better place for everyone."

Then she thanked the famous writer for spending time at the school.

Well, the same thing happened at another school.

THE END

CHAPTER FIVE

Ben the Warrior

In the pages of the US Army history there was a man whom own courage is what legends be. For Master Sargent Ben Kennisha of the 442nd division of WWII. He was a legend in that time who own bravery against so much odds. Just then disappeared right after the war, That brought out an Army historian to find out his story. From a wartime journal he kept and was certified by his own commander and this historian reads the very incredible story of courage and the greatest act of bravery from this one man.

It was in the month of June 1945
The place ---- Pacific Theater

I was in the wrong place way across the world, during this very ugly war. That has taken so many of my brothers and friends away. So, I became so determined to fight and avenge this very sad and dark time on me. When my CO found out that I was Japanese - American, He sent me to the back away from the fighting. It was a paperwork mess from HQ that placed me here.

I was so MAD at this one deal and I awaited for the right time to make my own move. So, one night I left everything behind me and went toward the Japanese lines and presented myself to the patrol on guard. I told them that I have lost my uniform and everything so close to me. That I wanted to fight so much, The patrol took me as a general and saluted me with highest honor. I could not take this act of kindness myself and ordered them to head back to the rear.

While back at the line, everyone there took me as a general. Then we was attacked by the American army and I was shot and dying from my fatal wound. My action saved lives and I never fired a shot even thou I was AWOL.

Well after the army historian read this final passage from this American hero. He went to his CO and read this story of honor. He sent it to the President and he in turned gave a long-awaited Medal of Honor to the family of Ben Kennisha.

For bravery above the call of duty against so many odds before him. In a dark time in American History.

THE END

CHAPTER SIX

MASTER

Introduction

This is a story of one man who had very incredible luck in a whitetail deer hunt in late November. For when he killed one super monster whitetail buck deer and winds up getting a very beautiful woman that also loves to deer hunt as well.

One year later and now his story needs to be told.

We meet a great man named Wendell Parks who was six feet five and around 300 and built well. This one man loved all alone hunting deer in the fall and winter. That was his pressure release from working on his new job. Ever since he had to give up playing pro football.

Now there was word spreading all around that a super monster whitetail buck was seen in the woods close by. Folks called him " Samson " for this one deer had a 28-inch height on his horns and closing in on being a 26-point buck. This deer would dressed out to be well over 400 lbs. of meat.

Wendell kept himself in shape and was very strong and walked fast. For in the cool mornings, he would train himself by pulling a weighted down sled uphill at his home. Then he got a new deer rifle an 45/70 Sharps reproduction rifle. This beautiful gun came to him as a gift , plus reloading supplies. He is very happy to received this gift from a close friend. He had made a custom gun case for the rare rifle out of red cedar wood that took him almost a month to make. Once done it was a great work of art. Then he learned how to reload all the ammo and placed online order to keep plenty of ammo in place.

Moments liked this brought out only the best in Wendell. Reloading ammo and dreaming about this future deer hunt. A lot of Wendell own relatives gave this man a very hard time about getting a whitetail deer.

But all he would ever say is "My time is coming" I will get a whitetail deer.

Then the relatives would ever only say "Sure Wendell Sure"!

DAY of the Hunt

It was upon a cold Sunday morning the time was 3 am Wendell went to a new spot in the woods. It was way up upon a hill and he got there at 4 am. He had a deer sleigh which held the Sharps rifle in place. This great man had a clear shot down hill to a open field. Because ammo for that one gun was so high, a mistake is not ok. This one shot had to be right and in his mind plan work on a way to leave. Unknown to him there was a very beautiful woman who also was on the other side of the hill. Looking down on the open field with a pair of binoculars she had on hand. Her hunting was so personal and wanted to change so much.

All this woman ever wanted was a photograph of the mighty " Samson ". Her name was Beebe Stranger and if she didn't get the deer photo due to things out of hands. She had a plan B also in mind, no deer well I am going to get a man.

This way my own relatives will leave me alone. My father wanted a son-in-law that also deer hunts and my brothers to have a deer hunting friend.

Beebe did get her picture of the mighty " Samson " and she was very happy. Then she heard a gunshot from a cannon of a gun. That made her drop down into a hole in the ground and then she said, " What the Heck is going on out there "! There was silence and then Beebe got her lady mirror and placed it on a stick. In the Y part of it and looked around very safe. Then came a big man who walked a ways from up the mountain. His one shot was over 750 yards away and it was true. Then he seen Beebe and said "Hello my name is Wendell and I can't believe that I got this one deer. Then he realized it was a super monster whitetail buck and not a mule deer. Which made him drop down on the ground and gave all his thanks to GOD.

Now my own relatives will leave me alone on deer hunting. Then Beebe said in silence, I am hoping that this one man is single. So, my own relatives will leave me alone as well. I was brought here to have peace in my family as well. Then Wendell got his prized Sharps reproduction 45/70 gun and put it in the custom gun case. That he made and got the massive whitetail buck on the deer sleigh. He look around for the best way to pull it to deer camp. Which was nine miles away on the route he was planning to go on. Beebe offered to help him pull on the deer, but Wendell made a mistake on his end by turning her down. This made Beebe very mad and it was right then, She made a life changing choice by walking in front of him taking off her orange coat. Just to reveal in front of him, that she was beautifully blessed and it was so very real.

Wendell apologized to Beebe for his own bad choice of words. Beebe accepted the apology and still had her own plan to help out. Now she alone said to Wendell

"If you can catch me then I am all yours for the night. We will have a date and hope many more but remember Wendell just one thing. I am very fast myself"

Wendell -------- "Dang I have my work cut out for me here"

Beebe went ahead of Wendell and just walked in front of him. This was the motivation that Wendell needed to pull this massive whitetail deer. This great man was also single and hoping that Miss Beebe is the same. Hoping to have her for a date of the highest honor and great respect. For any woman that loves to deer hunt is a treasure worth keeping and cherished.

THE LONG WALK BACK TO THE DEER CAMP I

Wendell and Beebe walked together and they began to talk. They had so much in common and that their parents who are also there hunting as well. Beebe parents and brothers were at one camp and Wendell's parents and brothers were at the other. This was a very positive family outing for both, Not knowing that two people lives was going to change forever.

Beebe Stranger and Wendell Parks for them it was a date. To be not forgotten between them. It was at Beebe deer camp where her brothers was giving a very hard time. When she came in and begin to talk to Ma and Me maw who were also there. For she was telling Me Maw that she got a big buck deer. When her brothers barge in and interrupted the talk. That got Me Maw very mad and she alone pulled out her own pistol at her nephews and made all of them. Take sudden notice, "never interrupt Me Maw when she is listening"!

They all backed off in a hurry and sit down fast. Then Beebe begin talking about getting a photograph of the mighty "Samson" the whitetail buck deer. Just passing by Wendell Parks came by and told Beebe that she was given credit for getting " Samson " . On the deer tag Wendell wrote Beebe name first before his own. This one move made everyone on Beebe side of the deer camp say.

"DAMM"

Beebe mom and Me Maw looked at her and said, "Darling you got a good man there, don't let him out of your sight." Beebe said ----------- " I won't "

On Wendell side of the deer camp all the relatives was starting to asked about one thing, "Did you get a deer Wendell"!

Wendell said, "Beebe Stranger and I got the mighty Samson ".

Sure, Wendell Tell us another tale, one relative said. Then Beebe walked in Wendell side of the deer camp. All the relatives were shocked by her appearance, and they had to take notice. Wendell 's grandmother was at the camp and told him. "Grandson" Don't let her go and cherish and treasure that beautiful lady. Wendell came back and said "Me Maw she is my best friend"

Those life-changing words by Wendell Parks changed Beebe and it was a good start for a friendship to grow. Now they are dating and as for the "Mighty Samson" the deer got mounted and is now on display. At Bass Pro shop who paid a very heavy amount of money for it. Beebe and Wendell sold the deer together to get a home.

For this one deer hunt changed the lives of two people who were there at the same time.

THE END

CHAPTER SEVEN

Dream World

What happens when you are dreaming of meeting that very special someone that makes you dream so very much, in which it takes over?

We meet a young man named Amos Winsted who alone had only one dream in life. That is to personally meet the very famous movie star "Fifi La Moure" She was a dark hair lady who was blessed and very lucky in life. But her own mansion needed yard work done and "Mr. Clyde", her groundskeeper, was very busy doing other things more important.

Which placed on Miss Fifi to get Clyde some help even for three hours' time. So, her manager went out and found a man named who was weed eating his own home and his name was Jay Winsted who own son Amos was out doing something else. The manager talked to Jay about weed eating a mansion. The pay was over $ 3,000 in cash and it was upfront and in advance. Jay looked at the cash and told the manager, "There is only one term on this future deal, I must teach my only son a lesson in life that he won't forget.

This got the manager to take notice and wanted to listen on the lesson planned out on young Amos. While Jay explained what was going on at the Winsted home.

My son took up a bad habit of cussing, and I tried to break him from it in the past and got placed in jail for my attempts. Which made us move away and settled here and begin a new life.

The Manager for Fifi came up with a plan and told Jay Winsted. This involves the groundskeeper Mr. Clyde and here is the plan just waiting to get your say on this. If your son works with Mr. Clyde and for every cussword that Amos says it will be a one hundred dollar fine for each word said out loud and in the open. Miss Fifi will be helping him quit also she will be teasing him and also teaching him a very dire lesson in life. Why she is helping you out Jay!

A while back you changed a tire on a car at the interstate, you never took any money for your honorable deed. In this car was Miss Fifi La Moure in the flesh and she is very thankful for your kindness. That was very rare these days and then you was gone. This really got to Miss La More and she so began to look for you. Now she wants to help you out in dealing with your son with honor. In the end Amos will not ever cuss or say very mean words out in the open. Jay agreed to the plan and he was going to be getting his son at the mansion at 1:00 pm today.

AMOS WINDSTED is now at the Mansion

It was right on time at 1:00 pm when Jay and Amos Winsted came at the movie star mansion. Then it happen Amos was in love with this movie star and he began to dream. About the romance and after hours that raised his pride to great heights. Then right after Jay his father left, the dream started to turn very sour when a older man named Mr. Clyde came up and woke up Amos and handed him two things. A weed eater that weighed like 20 lbs. and a bag full of already wound up weed eater spools. That his job was to weed eat the whole mansion which covered 35 acres and there was a steep hill that had over 100 statues on display. That also had to be weed eat as well. Amos got very serious mad and told " Mr. Clyde ", "NO WAY IN H" that I am going to do all of this. You got to be -------------------- Crazy.

Mr. Clyde had enough and he got Amos attention very fast and he said.

Amos, I have six thousand dollars in cash that I am going to give you after you do this job. Please remember one thing so very true with me. If you just say one cuss word or do a hand gesture you will lose 100 dollars fine for each word and 400 dollars for a hand gesture. Right now you are at $ 5,700 in cash. If you try to jump me for this money , I will kick your butt out of here. I used to be a navy seal but now I am retired and enjoy working for Miss Fifi and help keep this mansion in great shape. I am doing this favor to help out your dad because he saved my life back in the service. In the end you will never cuss or do a hand gesture out of hate.

Amos, who was surprised that his dream with Miss Fifi was now turning very sour. Liked a nightmare now without ending so soon. Yet the dreams of having a lot of money droved him to work. $1,000.00 hour was the source of good greed that was taking over this young man. All the weed eating was done now, and Amos was impressed by the speed of Mr. Clyde doing a job so very fast. Then he slipped and said another cuss word and wound up paying another fine of $100.00

A GOOD WOMAN BREAKS A MAN

Miss Fifi

She called Mr. Clyde to a very private meeting far away from Amos and there were more changes. Coming in regard to a Naked Garden of Statues that was on the grounds. That had to go because the statues were all sold and they had to be cleaned before leaving. Amos was looking forward to payday and going home and away from this nightmare of a day. Then Mr. Clyde called him in and showed off the naked garden of statues. There were fifty statues of a beautiful woman naked in all kinds of settings. This event set off another round of cussing from Amos and once more had to pay a fine.

Now it was setting into the very hard head of this young man. The hard fact was "No Cussing what's so ever is allowed" Now his money earned just took a two-thousand-dollar loss.

He was down to $3,000 dollars out of $ 6,000 to begin with at the first part of the day. Now Miss Fifi begins to talk outlines from an upcoming erotic movie, and it was a love scene, and her manager was helping her out on this. For Caleb this sour dream of his time was too much to handle alone. He was working well and loading up all the statues on the trailer that was parked. Miss Fifi said out one line from the movie and it broke Amos and he cussed a lot.

That's when Miss Fifi came to him and really lay it on the line. Amos ------------- " When you cuss out loud in public, People just don't care too much for it. You already lost $6,000.00 for a three-hour job. Think about it, my friend, I do have a surprise for you later. Well Amos Winsted did think it over and she was right as rain.

He came to Miss Fifi who was wearing a trench coat on now hiding all of her blessings. Amos apologized to her for his own bad mouth and was so ready to leave. Miss Fifi accepted the apology and gave Amos a present for his memory. For she opened the trench coat and knowing that this young man did not have a cell phone on him.

This lucky man just seen a measurement for all time. Miss Fifi was a 38kkk- 34 – 36. He started to stutter and became speechless, and his greater state was getting stronger. Then Miss Fifi closed the trench coat that was on her. She said "I done this to apologized to you and to make sure that you never cuss". I have a niece who is looking for a young man to take care of. She is very wealthy and you can call her a "Sugar Lady" please remember one thing, she does not like cussing at all. For if you say a bad word out in the open. She will leave you very fast and you will be broke.

Amos ----------- " OK "

Miss Fifi niece came in, and her name was Libby and she showed off her costume for an upcoming Halloween party. She was a French maid and Amos only said. "WOW"

Now a new man Amos Winsted never took up cussing ever again. When he came back home, Amos apologized to his parents, and they were both taken in. By the kind and very noble deed which was done. Amos and Libby {Miss Fifi niece} are dating and to this day now, Amos doesn't cuss anymore.

THE END

CHAPTER EIGHT

Romeo

We meet a young man by the name Juan Romeo who was on the brink of giving up. On life all around him, he was on a bad path, when his grandma step in and cornered her only grandson. Juan "What happen at school today"? He didn't want to talked about and this made his grandma very mad. So, she slammed him down to the ground and demanded a right out needing to know. Grandma used to be a wrestler who was a former Lucha Libre ladies champion and still kept herself in shape. It was fate that gave this one woman a grandson and it was a very beautiful gift. To receive this is what made her give up wrestling and raise Juan as her own.

Juan's grandmother was named Sable Marie Modula, and her wrestling name was the Silver Cougar. She was undefeated in the wrestling ring, and her title rein was short. She gave it all up to be with Juan Romeo. This was about 18 years ago when her only friend had a baby boy that was Juan. It was her last request that Sable will raise her son as a grandson. Sable agreed to this request and on that one night.

Then she went to be with GOD and wanted so much in the end.

That Juan would become a wrestler himself someday.

It was not happening because Juan wanted to do something else and that is to become a writer and preserve Latino Heritage. This was a noble and very cool thing that Juan always wanted to do.

Juan Romeo grew up in Texas and faced injustice a lot in school. Yet this young man never let hate turn his dreams away. Then on one night a very mean girl rejected him and by her horrible words she said. Did a lot of damage to this young man. It was about a week before his senior prom and when grandma found out.

Sable was so mad at the world and begin to work on a plan. While Juan went to do his homework and was alone for a spell, not knowing what his grandmother was up to. Now here was the Silver Cougar plan, "Revenge with Honor" as she called it.

So, she called in favors from other Latino ladies who wrestled in the past. "Just one thing please, have your nieces or granddaughters come to the senior prom and just say nice words to Juan"!

Some of the ladies didn't want to do this for Sable, but in the end a very rare social media post about the past would go online very fast. This made all the lady wrestlers in the past give in to the very simple request.

There would be over forty very beautiful ladies come into the senior prom. This was confirmed by email and phone calls. For Juan Romeo, his very own Senior Prom will be changing his life.

SENIOR PROM SATURDAY NIGHT AT THE HIGH SCHOOL NICE YOUNG MEN DO FINISHED FIRST

Juan Romeo was there at his senior prom and this time, His Grandmother was not there yet. He was alone in the corner facing a very hard and sad time. The jocks had their dates and took up the dance floor. Then one jock said a mean thing to Juan. "Nice guys like you don't ever finished first"!

These words hit harder than any fist or slam and no one should ever have this happen to them, but Juan kept his cool and wrote down a very great thing for his Latino heritage journal. Then there were beautiful women waiting to come in and all of them wanted to see Juan Romeo, some ladies drove over 200 miles one way and fours hours away. Every lady was a super knock out and very hot. There were some Latino ladies that made people say "WOW"

Because their own beauty made them take notice in a hurry. Each lady came by Juan's corner and gave him positive words of encouragement. That made all the jocks say a bad word which got the attention of the coach, and he did a lot of correcting them. Yet the jock said to him, the ladies are so hot and we all have to go now.

Then they left and soon all the ladies left that visited Juan except one. Her name was Leia Da Moore who is studying Latin American culture and heritage. She seen Juan and wanted to know more about him.

In the steps of highest honor and great respect at this beautiful moment.

Now it was just two people that was on the dance floor. Juan and Leia and it was very beautiful and special. After the dance was over they went on the different paths.

It was Leia that made the first move toward a beautiful moment . When she asked Juan out on another date.

MEANWHILE IN SABLE'S WORLD

She went to Juan's school and had a talk with the coach of the wrestling team. She was wanting to know just one thing. " Why they are any young women on the wrestling team "!

The Coach said in a bad way, " Girlie it's a man thing, Then the sup. who was in charge of the school called the coach to the office and gave him a very severe chewing out. Then they both walked back in and he apologized to Sable for his poor choice of words. Because this man valued his job and didn't want to lose it. Then the sup. had a idea for a future afternoon event.

A wrestling event to benefit the school, Wrestlers vs Faculty, everyone will win in the long run. Interest in this was very high for everyone and it drew in a lot of money. In ticket sales it was a sold-out event. The wrestlers wanted to do this show and all they asked for is faculty T-shirts. Then the wrestling coach wanted so much to do a mixed wrestling match. Man vs Woman to prove his point on the sport. There were no ladies that will take up on the challenge.

The coach was going to declare victory and keep women out of this sport. Then the school TV came on there was a challenger a woman who was masked. She said her name in Spanish and the very proud Latino students understood what is happening.

Silver Cougar is coming to the wrestling event to challenge you Coach.

If you win then there is a date with the Silver Cougar with highest honor.

But If the Silver Cougar wins there will be a women's wrestling team, she will be the teacher of that team.

This wrestling match to be drawn in a lot more interest on both sides.

Then it happen on a Saturday Night the main event. It was a mixed wrestling match between the Silver Cougar and Coach Adam Kimmel. The prize was a women's wrestling team to come in.

For Adam Kimmel a date with the Silver Cougar with highest honor that got to him very deeply. That brought out something from the Coach being in college sports to complete once again.

THE MATCH

It was a quick match for Coach Adam Kimmel for he was beat in less that 18 seconds. The Silver Cougar had her finishing move that pinned the Coach on the mat. Then on a following Monday Coach Kimmel had a great talk with his young men students. This man had to apologize for his choice of bad words. Then his boss came in with a masked lady wearing silver and talked in English this time.

Hello class, I am very proud to be a teacher of young ladies in wrestling. My name is the Silver Cougar, and I used to be a champion. I gave it all up so I can be there for my grandson Juan. That was 18 years ago and this was my best choice in life. The young ladies that showed up to learn about wrestling was so very proud to have this very famous pro wrestler, as a great teacher.

MEANWHILE

Juan Romeo and Leia begin their friendship by honoring Latino American heritage. This was a very positive move and now. They are dating to this very day.

All of this happens when a grandma stood up and change many lives by her actions.

THE END

CHAPTER NINE

MASTER

INTRODUCTION

In this new story we will learn about a Japanese/American woman with a hidden past. Who comes to the state of Missouri from Japan to begin a new life. After finding the right man who changes her life for the better. We meet Kari Akoto she is about 5 feet and 11 inches in height blonde hair and dark eyes. Her father was American and mother Japanese, her mother worked for a ninja master named Sensi Yasuko. At night she would clean the dojo and Kari learned all about this great man. Later in young Kari's life she begins to learn all about the martial arts. It was from her own mother talking about it for a way to let out anger.

This really got to Kari, and she wanted so much to know. This was against her mother's wish for her only daughter. But a darn cruel fate later on in life changed everything. When Kari's parents was killed in an automobile accident when she was 6 and having no family to go to.

Sensi Yasuko took this young girl in as his own and begin teaching her patience and when not to fight. This great man helped Kari grow up and become very smart in school and she only fight when it was a have to deal. Then on one night in Tokyo a man was getting beat up in a alley way by several bad men. Kari step in and took out all the bad men and saved the one from a cruel fate. The man saved invited Kari to live with him in the state of Missouri USA.

She took the invite and went with him to live a new life in the show me state. For learning more about her father heritage and a place in this world. It was right then that Kari learned more about her late father's place and now she wanted to be an American. Her journey into this new world would be life-changing and the greatest fight to be coming.

Kari new friend was named Malaki Del Wayne and he really loved this woman. In the matter of inside not out, because this one man never got excited on the outside. This really got to her, but it was Sensi told her that he was on the path of true love. That her heart needed to know more about this new friend.

So, Kari begin to learn all about Missouri and got herself a new ensemble of clothes and kept her past clothes hidden just for special occasions. The trip to Malaki's home in the Ozarks was a great one for her. For when was at his home there was two dogs that took a liking to her. Grumpy was the girl doggie and Cool One was the second. Both of them welcomed Kari in and for she had the sweetest voice.

That made two dogs fall in love with her as they guarded their new friend. Malaki was in a spot just to love what his own life be. Having a very beautiful woman in it now, Kari would be faced with a challenge that will define her in the end.

That challenge was in history when a new friend named "Ernie" needed help. To learn about it and maybe pass a test coming up soon in school. So, Ernie asked Ursa and she agreed to this very simple quest. To help him win a history quiz contest. The grand prize was a trip to a museum in Arkansas and a day out for two. Ernie wanted to go into this museum for himself, and Kari could take another person along. So Kari asked Malaki about this trip and he agreed to it. For this man wanted to do something very special for Kari out of love.

Later Ernie thanked Kari for her help on the history test in school. He passed it with flying colors and let Malaki know that Halloween night was coming up soon.

So, Malaki on Halloween night wanted to dress up and have a very positive night with Kari.

For when she heard of this noble idea from her love. It was a big YES, and she went and got her own costume.

It was a Ninja outfit, and it was snug on her and when Malaki seen it.

He closed the bedroom door and thanked Kari for making his day and this will be one beautiful night for the both of them.

THE END

CHAPTER TEN

Getting Caught

INTRODUCTION

Here is a set of four stories about love when either the gentleman or the lady.

Had to say just three words out in public. " I Love You "

That changes all lives at this time from the power of True Love.

FIRST COUPLE I

We meet this one couple Mari and Jeb DeLauro who own marriage is so rocky now. Because Mari was so dang busy working a lot to make it on top at her place of work. Jeb was busy at his own job that made him miss church on Sunday. Until one day at her place of work, she hears a beautiful poem spoken by her husband Jeb. In a desperate bid to win her hand with honor and deep respect. This poem takes her by surprise because Jeb never was any good in saying how he felt. He had to recite this one poem of deep faith and love, that makes her say out loud in Public and especially in a workplace. "I Love You"

Now here is the poem

Only One

When we meet and became one under the eyes of GOD

It was our own love for each other which became stronger through faith in him.

Through we have been through so many storms of our own past.

Now we will shine before him just to declare our true love.

That I alone love you Mari.

This one very short poem spoken by Jeb really touched Mari. For she alone was facing a cruel and hard time at her own place at work, Trying to talk out in a meeting with bosses. It was then she alone made a choice to leave her work for good. She raced out of the meeting and came to Jeb. Jeb " I Love You with all of my heart and soul.

Everyone in the workplace clapped their hands and cheered Mari for leaving.

That is so beautiful knowing that true love really shined today.

THE END

THE LETTER

42

Our second story takes place in modern time where a lady named Lori Danger gets a letter. From a man she has never meet and begins to think very hard about it. Well, The letter came from a faraway place and on the inside of this one such letter was a stamp envelope that was paid in advance.

The sender was hoping that Lori would be writing back to him. Well, she did write back to this mystery man then gets another letter that makes her think about a trip to see him in person. So she begins another letter and tells the Mystery man just one thing.

"I will be coming to see you, I will be close by and then drive a rental car."! Then her mystery man writes back and gives her a paid airline ticket and money to spend for this trip. Then he writes in a note to remember "If you do come to see me, your life will be changed" But if you decline my offer and not come to see me.

Then you will be stuck in place and be all alone. But Lori went with her first choice and decided to go and find this mystery man. Who all alone made her day with the very first letter that she read. For this one man had very beautiful penmanship which made her begin to love this man.

Well, she made the trip and landed in Arkansas and droved the rental car. To the town of Dash Missouri which didn't exists on any maps. Now this young woman was getting very mad at life and made a choice now to leave Arkansas, and head back up to Missouri and take the next flight out. Then the rental car she was driving broke down just right in the hollow where there was no cell phone service.

Lori Danger was getting so hot at life, and she begin walking up a very steep hill. Maybe to get cell phone service and leave so fast. It was there at the top she seen a crew of men working on building a house. There was one man in this group took notice of Lori and he alone approached.

Then He said, "You must be Miss Lori Danger"

Lori replied, "How do you know of my name, I have never seen or heard from you ".

Just then another man came up to Lori and taken his jacket off and presented himself. "Miss Lori Danger here is your new pickup to drive and it's all yours."

Lori ------------ Now it's getting very weird here. Then the second man took off his shirt and Lori just seen the most beautiful man in her world and begin to have problems. She wanted to cuss and say things out loud but all she could say is "I Love You and I want to know you", " WOW "

This really floored the man and now he presented himself in a proper way.

My name is Clint and I own this new home, and I was with your late brother in that ugly war. He talked about you with highest honor and great respect. Then he was gone and I missed him so very much. I made a promise to him to take care of you. Your brother told me that you like a 1956 ford pickup and wanted to drive one. "Well, here is your truck to drive for yourself!

Lori ------------ Thank You and can we have another date, I really want to know you more.

Clint was surprised and everyone begin to leave for the day. All that was left was just Clint and Lori in the new home. Lori Danger just shut the door and said " Let us have this talk in private".

THE END

Our Third Tale is all about " When a Hot Wheel car grows up "

    We meet this couple Adam and Mari Towles who were doing good on money. Now we go first with Adam Towles who alone loved old cars and comic books. It was the love of comic books that he meet Mari at a Comicon convention. They dated for three years and got married on Superman's birth month in June. At first their marriage was going great and then it got rocky in a hurry. Adam had problems in expressing his love for his wife. Because Mari wanted so much to hear from Adam say out loud in public setting.

"I love You Mari"

    She was sensing trouble from Adam and went to her brother Luke to help get a vintage car. There was a vintage car auction and this woman had the money to spend. Luke took up this invite for it was a dream of his that was coming true. This man had only one condition that he too can get a vintage car or pickup.

    Mari said " Yes of course you are not coming home without having one in your hand "!

    The Car Auction was coming and Adam Towles had to miss it due to his busy work . He told Mari go and have fun at it. Then Mari told Adam one thing that sounded not right to him.

"Adam I am going to make this one hot wheel grow up to be a real car ".

Adam Towles ----------------- "Mari you are nuts and if you do by fate make that hot wheel grow up "

"I will say to the whole world that I Love You in public"

Mari Towles ---------------- " You are on and it will happen and I will even test your devotion to me. For I know of my girl friends that are super hot and I am going to introduce them to Cosplay.

Adam Towles left for his job not realizing what have just happen. Unknown to him about the vintage car show there was his all time favorite car . That was up for sale it was a 1959 Cadillac series 62 fully restored and ready to drive. The news made him very sick and upset at the same time. Then his work day was not good for Adam could not get his mojo a going. Then after work he went to a bar and call a cab in advance. Because he was not driving home drunk. The cab company took him close to home and he fell into a ditch. Mari Towles was ready to spring her trap and make her husband say just three words in public. Mari even got her girlfriends into this bold plan.

Mari's very hot girlfriends got into Cosplay at a comic book convention for the grand prize was 5,000 dollars in cash. Now there was four ladies wanting to do this and being with Mari was also a plus.

For 1,000 dollars pay just for one hour of work at a comic con convention was just way too hard in pass it up.

For this was a quest of honor and great pride in all. In Mari's spot it was hearing from her husband just three words in public . That means so much to her, Well Adam had just passed out in a ditch in front of her home.

Began to draw attention from the neighbors and now Mari's plan comes to be.

She called her brother to drive the 59 Cadillac and place the car over the ditch to cover up Adam.

Because she was getting dressed up with her hot girlfriends.

To begin teaching her husband a very important thing. That a good woman needs to be cherished and respected so much. Mari even gave up her future share of the comic con money and gave it all to the four very hot girlfriends. The ladies helping Mari out got a 250 dollar boost for the one hour pay.

While under the vintage car Adam Towles begins to wake up with a deep hangover on him. He begins to think things out and realizes that he married a very beautiful woman in Mari his wife. The he hits his on a car muffler that was still hot and says "ouch", for his own choice of words was a price he pays just to keep a supermodel type of wife. Then he crawls out of the ditch and stands up just to see so many people looking at him. Never knowing that a vintage old car is right in front of him.

Then Adam sees eight women all wearing long jackets and boots. There was two ladies coming at him, It was then which he alone made a life choice decision.

LORD JESUS IF THIS IS MY BEAUTIFUL WIFE MARI coming at me, I need to say what is on my mind right now.

"Mari Towles, I LOVE YOU WITH ALL OF MY HEART AND SOUL"!

Suddenly two hundred people have gathered around the vintage car and they all began to clap. Their hands in a most beautiful moment in the neighborhood.

Adam and Mari Towles renewed their love and the vintage Cadillac was the seal of true love.

Well Mr. Adam Towles never doubted his wife ever again . For this one lucky woman made a hot wheel grow up to be a full size car.

THE END

Now our fourth and our very last story is called The Fighter

Introduction

In this story we meet a young man named Aesop Majors who was given by birth a rare name. Who grew up in the state of Georgia and learn all about respect and great honor. From his grandfather named Atticus who alone told him the ways. In getting a right woman is thru deep respect and honor.

To all women in life because it was in the right way of a gentleman. But in Aesop's world he was a really a super rare kind of young man.

A Southern Gentleman in modern times

Aesop grew up in the state of Georgia along with his grandfather Jay and his grandmother June. They wanted their only grandson to respect women and always have honor. In doing this very rare and noble quest , It seems to be impossible when women in Aesop age were so very different.

"Like they were all snubs" ---------------------Aesop Majors once said.

Yet it was his grandparents made him be so true in Southern gentleman ways and they got thru to him in the early years growing up. Aesop was very fast with his hands and when he had to fight. He used his smarts over a fist anytime but when at the very last resort. He was undefeated but made a promise to never fight to his grandparents.

This would be a bitter mistake on his end for Aesop. Because love came to him in a beautiful lady named Lura Wayne and she was going to be a Hollywood movie star. Aesop Majors pursue her with highest honor and respect. But this woman wanted nothing to do with him. Then there was a bitter fight that took Aesop down and he had to leave with valor.

Lura Wayne changed her name to Amanda Means that was her stage name. Now that Aesop was out of the picture for good. She focused on her career without any luck. Now that her life took a very serious and sharp turn to the worst. When no one wanted her in any movies or TV show. This was very bad and the truth came out. That one ex-boyfriend posted videos of her without consent in a bitter revenge and then took his life for the final blow. Just to avoid jail time and this brought out Lura's me- maw to visit Hollywood.

It was only then that this movie star to be had a long talk with her me-maw. This old woman who retired from the Navy with honors begin telling about Aesop Majors. At first Lura never wanted to hear anymore talk about Aesop. Then she called for her manager and agent they didn't come to help.

Me-maw ------------ "I 've told both of them that my talk with you is private and not to come in. Because I will use a major can of "Whoop ASS " on both of them. Whenever Lura heard " Whoop Ass " growing up it was very serious. For her Me-Maw trained Navy Seals while in the navy before retiring and raising a family.

Lura Wayne left Hollywood on that one day and came back home. Only to find out that the family farm was going to be sold so close to Christmas and this really soured her spirit. It was on December 20th the date of the sale and the auctioneer was so sad for doing this. There was a lot of people there so closed to 600.

Her family farm was closed to 500 acres of flat land and it faced a slow slope uphill.

There were farmers there trying to block the upcoming sale but they had to give up. Then a limo pulled up and watched this horrible thing being done. Then the Auctioneer got a very important phone call.

That the farm was bought lock stock and barrel everything was paid in full. The sale was stopped and people came around that no good limo thinking that a big box retailer was coming in.

Hate came over them and then a two big men came out and they fired a loud shotgun into the air. The place got quiet fast. Then a lone young man came out and he had a very important paper with him.

His name was Aesop Majors and new owner of this farm, Lura was shocked that this man whom she rejected and told off several times in the past. Comes back into her world on the darkest hour.

He wanted to talk to Lura's mother and father and brothers who were there present. He had something to say and then leave with honor and great respect. "Folks, I gave up my wealth just to this one thing and that is, to buy this farm for Lura's mother and father. Here is the final payment and there is a copy of it. I wanted to give you a mortgage burning party."

"Lura, I wanted to say this from my heart and soul, that I Love You very much. If you want to be with me, I will treat you with the highest respect and deep trust. I am going to be your neighbor and if you ever decided to give up Hollywood. You will always be welcome in my small home. I don't know what you did online and just don't care. For every day I am with you is Christmas for me. The best gift I have ever receive is you."

"Lura Wayne, I Love You"

Everyone at the auction was clapping their hands for they were a witness to something beautiful. Lura Wayne went after Aesop and ran and chased him down to the ground. Then she said "Aesop Majors you are a good man and I am going to stay with you", "only Death will breaks us apart, Just to be together in Heaven. This is the most amazing thing you have done."

THE ENDING

Lura and Aesop went dating and in a year got married. She gave up Hollywood cause she has found happiness that her heart yearns for. Aesop became a big part of her family and it took courage for him to say just three words in a large public event. He gave up his wealth and found something greater.

LOVE